Love Among
the Tombstones

Florence Hackman

Copyright © 2010 Florence Hackman

All rights reserved.

ISBN 1-145-370813-8

EAN 13 9781453708132

Inkhorn Press

PO Box 519

Edgewood NM 87015

For Danny

Contents

Tombstones I 9

Tombstones II 10

Tombstones III 11

To a Connecticut Farmer 12

Dreaming 15

Nine To Five 16

If Only The Doughnuts Were Not Soggy 17

No More Talk 18

Comment On a Career—the 1970's 19

Fire and Casualty and Wallace Stevens 20

Waiting 21

Equations 22

Unrealized Capital Gains 23

Calculating 24

Unconglomerated 25

Searching 26

Your Book 27

Impulses 28

Front Door 29

Promises 30

Interim 31

Dialogue In a Beer Parlor 32

Lost 33

Lament of One Generation 34

The Tourists 35

Remainder Man 36

Yesterday 37

Last Night 38

Absurd 39

Carter's Cotton Pants 40

Santa—Depression Revisited 41

Betrayal 42

Wake 43

Departure..44

Prepare Yourself for Death...45

Lament of an Out-of-Work Actor..................................46

Simply...47

Too Late..48

Trivia...49

Chatham Break..50

Tides 51

When I Was Young..52

The Inevitable End of Emptiness...................................53

Legacy...54

War Games—I...55

War Games—ll 56

Egrets..57

Nickel Ice Cream 58

Whimsy..59

Tombstones I

The hour comes again. I wait each year
For recognition of a fruitless deed.
That I may say the time is now and here,
Summon an audience to my stark need.
The caravans are passing near the gate.
They left no gifts behind, no precious myrrh.
The mourners came, their coming was too late,
Their tears a pittance, their prayers obscure.
And my weak blood was drawn out of the vein.
I did not flinch but turned a rigid chin,
And watched my birth and death dissolve in rain,
And took the final judgment of my sin.
The hour passes marking off my death.
I marvel that I am allowed to breathe.

Tombstones II

There is no simple silence for regret
Of seven years, not famine and not feast.
The hunger of a life is now increased
While hirelings of conscience stand erect,
Their pistols held in violent hands no threat,
When Sundays are like Mondays, West is East,
And the whole globe a sour cake of yeast,
And lovers never wept and never met.
The canvas heart half painted and half wet,
The morning tears of April now unleashed.
The virgin maid silent and unappeased,
The world in one fantastic pirouette.
The little dancer has worn out her shoes.
And last night Hamlet missed all of his cues.

Tombstones III

My life has been lived without memories,
Not looking back into the empty room
That houses ghosts in minor travesties.
The bride is dead and buried is the groom.
I have no roses pressed into a book,
No claim to wilted lilacs in the spring.
The pool is muddy, dry the autumn brook
That hugged the pebbles that I used to fling.
And I am I at any time of year,
Not peasant, king or great man of affairs,
I wash my face, I drink my sour beer.
I sleep in beds and sometimes sit in chairs.
I had a dream last night that made me cry.
I saw a bearded Moses with one eye.

To a Connecticut Farmer

Silver bars are laid in the old French well.
The tarnished age of handicraft
And homely needs
Again brought to mind.
The stone house on a Connecticut hill,
Erected while the farmers laughed,
Plucked their weeds,
Laid finger to the wind,
And gone is the brutal city,
The elastic age of complex tragedy.

The analysts lie in wait,
The vultures of lost childhood,
Crying escape,
Though the trees are felled,
The apples sprayed,
The rough ground tilled.

Here only the hurricanes can find entrance.
The uninvited stand outside the gate.
A man's beard can grow long
A man's arms strong,
For gone is the maddening tick
Reminding us the hour is late,
And gone is absurd romance.

The fields, the trees, the earth remain the fact,
Absolute, secure, unchallenged in being.
All damage is unintentional,

All growth unconventional,
From the living and seeding
Nothing can detract.
Old Watrous views the digging of the well,
With grand impatience saying not a word.
He dug his own fifty years ago.
He thinks the young man's digging goes too slow,
The young man's method openly absurd.

Only the old man's eyes will tell
That ancient backs are stronger still.

Old Watrous turns back up the hill.
He stops and sits down on a stone
And views his neighbor now alone,
Unschooled in all but will.

Questions will be asked. Will the crops grow?
Will spring be late this year? Will crows return?
Will storms come on a summer night?
And winter snow?
The Georgics still hold true
For cows are slow
In evolution.

The pioneers are back from the West,
And back from the plain,
East where the first rock was upturned.
All lessons have been lived and learned
And will be learned again
Before the weary seek their rest.

Here is a mountain, here a sea,
And a long deserted brook,
And one ear of corn solemnly
Hanging from the tallest stalk.
A pasture and a deer print,
A swallow's nest still hidden,

An evergreen, a sprig of mint,
A black crow come unbidden,
    And a weary tale of woe
Lost in the earth,
Lost in the seed,
Lost in the everlasting
Living and dying.

Trials absolute and sentences obscure,
The East the essence in all literature.
Callous hands groping in the dawn
For agonies of love now gone
Now past for past is pure.

Under a stone, any shapeless stone,
The crawling things find home
And still are moving to a distance
Led by ever-gloating chance.
Each man is found unwanted and alone.

Dreaming

All my lovers are now too old
To do the things they were meant to do.
I walk in the sand and pick up white stones
And watch the sun rise and lie under the dunes.
So why this dull aching and why are there tears?
I'm past the age of hearts breaking and counting the years
Of dreaming and wishing and feigning.

Nine To Five

I have watched in the mornings and afternoons
The men, who sit restless in swivel chairs,
Running manicured fingers through stray gray hairs
And growing as big as ten-cent balloons.
1 have heard them whistle their hopeless tunes,
Denouncing too boldly frivolous cares.
Ah, the refuge they take in worn-out airs,
The comfort they seek in a dish of prunes.
The ripe cataracts are turning them blind.
The once sharpened pencil is but a stub.
The man to my right is itching behind.
He can't move himself, not even to rub.
Yesterday, poor Clarence went out of his mind.
He drowned himself in a lavender tub.

If Only The Doughnuts Were Not Soggy

If only the doughnuts were not soggy,
I could take saccharin in my coffee,
Politely smile when the men are stuffy,
Appear alert when I'm really foggy,
If only the doughnuts were not soggy,
What worlds would be mine by half past the hour.
Old Crowe could pick at his teeth forever
Without turning my weak stomach sour,
Or giving a thought to my delicate liver.
If only the doughnuts were not soggy
1 might see the sun through the window shade,
Feel the breath of morning only outside,
Forget that I work because I am paid
And carry through with today's masquerade,
If only the doughnuts were not soggy.

No More Talk

No more talk in the middle of the day,
Let the window cleaner hang from the ledge.
Gauguin's in Tahiti and I'm in jail
Or whatever you call a square-foot cage.

No more thought in the middle of the day.
Let a staple fire the copying machine.
Schweitzer's in Africa and I grow pale
Or whatever you call the color pain.

No more work in the middle of the day.
Let the old man buzz until he is blue.
Steinbeck's east of Eden, and I've grown stale
Or whatever you call it when you're through.

Comment On a Career—the 1970's

In a shoe box on a shelf letters written
During the War are carefully preserved.
Reminders of a love hidden from the world.
Passion on a page is safe enough.
And now I address myself
To making money, a humorless pursuit
To which I am ill-suited though infinitely successful.
Mistakes are calculated in dollars that buy nothing.
My admiration is restricted to bandits
Who shun the written word.
It is an absurd pastime. Compound interest
Never warmed a bed, and life's paradox
Cannot be clarified by bonds and stocks.
God I am lonely. It is two in the morning.
The market opens at ten.
And life begins again.

Fire and Casualty and Wallace Stevens

I say his room is no longer his room,
That walled off space in a place of commerce.
His name is not legend, his song a tune
Unwhistled, empty as an empty purse.
The corridors dark though the morning light
Breaks eastward over the last evergreen.
Not one sweet soul to whisper good night,
Not one voice to echo the old man's dream.
It was among strangers he penned his way,
With cold good mornings in parentheses.
The sonnets came at the end of a day
Like apple pie served with a square of cheese.

Now all my credentials have been furnished,
What more then is needed to be published?

Waiting

I have waited too long to tell old friends
The days they made mine assuaged the grief
Of terror-etched dreams borne without relief
And a life lived sans means and choked with ends.

It was too late last night, even later today.
I put a nail in the coffin
And then set to work carving a puffin
As if death were a trivial matter.

So what do you do at four in the morning
When chimneys are leaking and rooms are cold,
And no club and no cause are worth joining,
And all stocks and bonds and houses are sold.

Equations

These are days without grace.
Equations now are more complex,
And dignity escapes the day.
Mornings continue gray affairs,
And evenings pass with no prayers
Said. Those who once were gay
And none could vex
Are absent. In someone's place

A robot sits and does not smile.
The blood of vandals marks the herd.
A way of warmth is out of style
And all but agonies absurd.

Unrealized Capital Gains

For too long the leaves have fallen.
Rust lies heavy on the hinge.
Unripe still the watermelon
Empty as the western range.

Say a good word for tomorrow,
Cackle in the morning sun.
Mend the wings of injured sparrows,
Journey forth to Avalon.

Death is in a neighbor's house,
Well contained and not contagious.
Gold is in the hands of Faust,
Profits sweet and so outrageous.

Calculating

While I waited for my healers
I put death on hold,
Then entered my life in a computer
Listing what I bought and sold.

The machine printed "error"
Reenter if you can.
I followed the instruction
But there was no tape to scan.

I had fallen through the cracks
Between the letters A through Z.
And the computer printed clearly
That I wasn't really me.

Get a word processor, they said
And add a fax machine.
I answered, I'm - too old
To have machines trash every dream.

Unconglomerated

Gallant and grim, not marked by shame or worn
By all the shabby ways monies dictate,
Not marked, not bangled, not the least absurd.
A lazar in the desert fully cured,
Now holy in a world of heat and hate,
With time to love and time to think and mourn

For winter snow that covered Walden Pond,
Lost lamaseries on a mountain side,
Eden before the fall of everyman,
Utopia sans pestilence and pain,
The knightly quest that won the virgin bride,
And truth above the dollar and the pound.

Searching

I have looked for my lost child
In oceans far away from home,
On wooded mountain sides, on city streets,
On ice flows in the South and North
Poles far apart. I sought my worth
And found an emptiness too awful to describe.

Your Book

I hold in my hand a book
You once owned, neatly penned
Notes decorate each page.
And now when I read the lines
Written by poets known to every school boy,
I think of all you could have done
And never did. And when I look
To decipher the old mysterious blend
Of works created by the Greek sage

That beckoned Keats and Shelley to drink wines
And celebrate odes that told of joy
And love of maidens they won
In battles with the muse.

Impulses

I sit in my chair and wait for things to happen.
They never do.
Big things, little things are all a piece.
And the shapes are odd and few
To give me the much wanted release
From doubts and devils that plague
My every day.
And then I wait for
Thoughts that dominate and vague
Impulses that make the front door
Open and close for any thief
Who dares to enter unannounced.

Front Door

Something inside of me is missing.
Passion, love, the urge to cry,
For all dreams shattered
By a devilish wind
That split trees in two.
I think of what once mattered
In my life—a gentle breeze
That set me free to do battle.
And, I alone, at one or two in the morning,
Creep down the stairs and open
The front door to welcome nothingness.

Promises

Childhood was a game
Played under crabapple trees
And blueberry bushes
Laughter and spankings
Among the slobbering kisses
Of ancient aunts and uncles
Who came to call.

But that's not all.
Childhood was promises
Long forgotten by senators
Who dished out metaphors
And lame excuses for all the abuses
Of governments.

Interim

I wish I could write simply,
Simply about my life, my love,
My loathing of the mundane.
Simple was never meant to be.
It's not my way, nor
The style of anyone I admire.
A grim unfeeling face is all I see,
My face in the mirror,
My chin stuck out,
And eyes quite blank.
And what beauty there once was
Is now buried in the mud wrought
By yesterday's torrential downpour.

Dialogue In a Beer Parlor

Do you know how often you talked of light
And dark as if a painting were all you
Had in mind, shunning the chiaroscuro
Of the erratic self lost in the fading shadow
Cast by words as burdensome as excess freight.

And then you talked of bare walls, clean sheets
Of paper, portraits and novels, seascapes,
Dialogues in labyrinths where no maps
Drawn have taken you. You drew the fine lips
Hollow eyes and hair of ancient Greeks,

Set them to dance in synagogues of self,
Rhymed them with tragedy and turned your face
Now wrinkled with horrors of too much choice,
Too many novels, operas in the place of life.
Then passionless, your word was death.

Lost

Lost in a world of words so long,
I hear no voice, no human sound.
Reality is on a page,
The covers of a book my cage.

I lost my April long ago.
No spring can ever bring her back.
Tomorrow is a lonely play.
The script was written yesterday

When lips still moved and eyes still saw
The blooming dogwood in the yard.
And springtime promised much too much
Beyond all sound, and sight and touch.

Lament of One Generation

It is not that frontiers have long vanished
Or worlds are stale and afternoons a bore,
Or courage a feckless emotion or war
A manufactured evil. Undernourished

Breadline boys of yesterday now dismiss
The siring of a brood of parasites.
The plenty not the poverty ignites,
And freedom's definition is a hiss.

Scion will not be strangled with his sire.
The sons desert Laocoön with joy.
The academe is dubbed another Troy,
And able-bodied young prepare the pyre.

The Tourists

Past all the bridges, all the monuments
Of East and West,
The challenge of the chimera,
The cries of' heron
Lead the pack.
The harbor in the fog
Where termites feast
Sinks into black,
And travelers jest.

No lonely voyagers these,
With pockets full,
They charge the ocean,
Swift dynamos,
Tourists of the seven seas,

Waiting for the Carthaginian rise,
For queenly Didos dancing nude,
The trinkets of Egyptian marts
And Pharaoh's tomb.

Some time in Paris which I've never seen,
In winter, spring or fall,
In an unknown cafe
Where absinthe is the order of the day
Not just for Mr. Hemingway,
I'll have a ball.

Remainder Man

I heard last night that Sweeney died.
A peaceful death so I was told.
So what, I said, can you deny
His body now is cold.
And only one thing he was spared.
The agony of growing old.

I heard last night that Totten died.
A painful death so I was told.
So what, I said, can you deny
His body now is cold.
He gained so little in this life
Not even growing old.

I heard, I don't remember when
That every one I knew had died.
Useless deaths, so I was told.
So what I said, can you deny
Their bodies now are cold.
And I am left alone to grieve
And suffer growing old.

Yesterday

There is so much I have forgotten,
What life was like during the.war,
The summer I picked blueberries
On the hill, and so much more.
The lovely nights he held me in his arms.

How could I forget I had a lover?
Not just a lover but a friend
Who introduced me to the piping plover
And days with no beginning and no end.
And life with no questions and no qualms.

Last Night

Last night? Was it last night or the night before?
Or days ago or months or years?
Time was never my strong point.
The strain of remembering is too great.
And memories themselves a weight
I cannot bear. The fears, too many to recount,
Grotesque as tablets crashing down the Mount.
Betrayal, that's a word that sums up all my shattered
dreams.
Not your betrayal but my own
That stupidly allowed your schemes
To violate my innocence.
And now at night, I am left alone to mourn
The havoc of last night's vicious storm.

Absurd

My childhood was lived on a comparative basis.
What they had, what we had.
When I think about it, which I seldom do,
It was not so bad,
Not having what they had.
Sad but not so bad.

So being deprived of plenty,
I never learned the meaning of envy,
A dirty word in an absurd world
Of nothingness.

Carter's Cotton Pants

I now know why I was never
            invited to a dance.
It wasn't my hairdo or lipstick
But my Carter's cotton pants.

While other girls wore satin and silk,
And were dressed to the hilt.
I wore my Carter's cotton pants
Even though I had no kilt.

I wore cotton pants throughout childhood.
And even wore them to France-
Wondering what they would say
            On the Rue de la Paix
To my Carter's cotton pants.

And now when I think back
To the dates I once had,
Beneath my frocks and permed locks,
It was not merely by chance
That I had on my Carter's cotton pants.

I wore cotton pants when I was married.
And it will certainly not be by chance,
That when I am finally buried
It will be in Carter's cotton pants.

Santa—The Great Depression Revisited

It was tag we played
And hide and seek.
The nights were cold,
The days were bleak.
But we drove the big ripper
Down every steep hill
When the snow was piled high
And cushioned each spill.

To say that childhood was sweet
Would be telling a lie.
We didn't stop to think
And were too busy to cry.
They were the rich ones,
And we were the peasants.
No Christmas for us,
No tree and no presents.

And so in December
And in January too,
I feel downright wretched
And forever blue.
That was so in my childhood
And true now that I'm old.
There's no warmth in my heart,
And my hands are so cold.

I've never grown up.
I feel pinched and small,
And keep on waiting
For Santa to call.

Betrayal

How easily you spoke each word,
As if you meant what you said.
And I believed, yes, I believed,
My head was buried in the sand
Of some lost desert. You waved a wand
And myth and magic achieved
What I could not. I was afraid
Of nothingness and all the absurd
Fantasies you conjured in your head.

You introduced me to deceit
And laughed at what you had done.
And knowingly you crushed a dream
And left me on a distant shore,
My world in shambles, incomplete,
My life sullied to the core.
And now, I struggle to redeem
The pieces strewn, and what is more
1 long to be forever clean
From all betrayal and your commands
That bind me with your brutal hands.

Wake

They only mourn the young, and now that I am old
No one will weep for me or keep me from the cold
Ground that awaits my shriveled bones.
I shall die alone, and all songs sung will be for others.
And the plates set at the wake, plates filled with scones
And other choice fare, will be eaten by those
Who will not shed a tear.

Snow fell last night, silent as it fell.
Silent as I will be in my death.

Departure

I remember what life was like
Before I had a double chin.
Before I learned to speak
Of rogues and rags and sin.

Not any sin, but sin delicious
And promises they could not keep.
Ambassadors of evil, so officious,
Despising me, denying sleep.

Not only sleep, but days and nights.
And now the silence descends
And sweeps away all human rights,
Confusing means, destroying ends.

Politicians squirm and prattle,
And offer platitudes absurd.
They send a nation into battle,
Armed not with truth. A helpless herd

Runs wild both in the West and East,
And kills the dream, but not the beast.

Prepare Yourself for Death

Prepare yourself for death he said
In no uncertain terms.
Excise your soul, I'll take control
And feed your body to the worms.

Was it Satan who so directed
That I should not be missed?
With knife in hand, he dissected
My life and all the ends I missed.

I shall not plead, I shall not cry
For trumpets silent in the sky.
Tra la la la and hi-dee-ho.
I think it's time for me to go.

Lament of an Out-of-Work Actor

I beg at last to he heard.
That's all I'll ever want.
A chance to have my say.
A request to some, absurd,
Who judge the last word
Of one who dares to flaunt
His role as Hamlet in a play
That failed both on and off Broadway.

I beg at last to be seen.
That's all I'll ever ask.
A chance to show what I can do
And prove at last what might have been,
An actor, strong and bold and lean
And always equal to the task
Of eloquence and derring-do
And strong of spirit when he's through.

I beg at last to stay the course,
That's all I'll ever seek.
A chance to climb the highest wall
Or battle an opposing force
And say the lines until I'm hoarse,
And baritone becomes a squeak.

I beg and beg and that is all
Until the script begins to pall.

Simply

I wish I could write simply,
Simply about my life, my love,
My loathing of the mundane.
Simple was never meant to be.
It's not my way, nor
The style of anyone I admire.

A grim unfeeling face is all I see,
My face in the mirror,
My chin stuck out,
And eyes quite blank.
And what beauty there once was
Is now buried in the mud wrought
By yesterday's torrential downpour.

Too Late

I think back to the time
We were spared a winter storm.
Storm is too tame a word.
It was a hurricane that stopped
Before it reached our door.
The lights flickered. The wind was strong,
Strong enough to down the great oak
That covered the front yard.
A hurricane that butchered leaves.
Two titans battled for survival,
The storm that surely could not last,
The tree that lasted far too long.

And now it is too late,
Too late to write the perfect poem,
The classic tale of birth and death,
Too late to sit and patiently await
The lifting of the darkness.
I should put down my useless pen
And cry myself to sleep again.

Trivia

Little sorrows keep creeping in to mar my day,
Nothing momentous.
The loss cf a lover, the death of a child,
A house swept into the sea.
Everyday things when one thinks of the world.

A bore if you force someone to listen.
What can anyone say'?
That the wind last night was wild,
Indeed calamitous.
How high the price for being free,
Incalculable and absurd.

Chatham Break

All the names are run together
And flow as a river flows.
I cannot tell one from the other
Despite the marks and flaws.
So what call you a magnolia
That blooms in the wintertime?
And what say you of an azalea
To which you can lay no claim?

I feel like a fallen petal
Like a dove no longer white.
And the day that was once so special
Has disappeared into night.

There's a break that has let in the ocean
And the threat of a tide too high
That will sweep away the sands
And leave nothing but a sigh.

I shall wait 'til the moon is full.
I shall wait for the sands to recede.

And perhaps when I feel the last pull,
I shall drown in my sorrow or bleed.

Tides

I shall walk outside myself and shed my depression
So a new skin can grow.
A set of armor plates that barbs cannot penetrate.
And when I am weighed down
I'll strip again and walk into a sea so calm
And welcoming,
Where sorrow has no place, and memories are lost
In tides, now high, now low.

When I Was Young

When I was young, I spent my days
Writing about flowers and death
Or halcyon days or winter storms.
Cosmic events, so I thought.

And now I'm old, I still write
About flowers and death and
Golden wreaths and ice that
Covers my front walk,
So thick, I dare not venture out.
And that's what life is all about,
Flowers and death and winter storms.

I cannot see the harm in all that
Nature has dealt out.
I wish I had other themes
To occupy my time.
Instead I dream my useless dreams
And bury them in rhyme.

The Inevitable End of Emptiness

I did not attempt suicide.
He did.
I did not drink myself into oblivion.
He did.
Together we were nothing. Apart,
Mere shadows struggling
Toward the inevitable end of emptiness.

And now after so many years,
I cry for my lost love
And all the promises of youth we trashed.

Legacy

Your legacy to me a poem crafted with care
And honed to perfection as only you could do
I read and weep and weep and read
And hang on every word you wrote.
You taught me the rightness of grief
On nights so dark, when all I need
Are linens to cover my pain,
And no light to injure sleep.

And which of us is better off'?
You in death
Or I weighed down by years
Of emptiness and stupid tears.

War Games—I

I lost my lover to the war.
What more can I say?
I can't remember which war it was.
Why it was fought and for what cause.
But I remember the hour and the day
Death knocked too loudly on my door.

My unborn children have no headstones
And mock me in my barren state.
I wander through the arid fields
That offer nothing, and their yields
Are worthless as my grief and life alone.

I dream of what might have been
Had he lived to claim my love.
And all reality is now obscene,
With hawks devouring each white dove.

War Games—II

How goes the war? the old man asked.
Were many men killed today?
And what about the little child
Left naked in at pile of mud?
Was every soldier assigned a task
Now unfulfilled? Who now holds sway
Over empty fields and the wild
Drowned by a flood
As fierce as carried Noah's ark
To lands unchartered?

Is God still on our side? the young boy asked.
Why were so many killed today?
And what about the little child
Left orphaned in an empty town?

Whose war is it? the widows asked.
And decked the graves with wilted flowers.
And demagogues clasping idiot cards
Read it's theirs, not ours.

Egrets

Once again, the month in my memory
Comes hack to haunt,
Not the age of chivalry
Or the year of want.
Not the warm breeze
Touching my brow,
Not the sweet peace
The gods will not allow.
The days now number thousands,
Strong like a herd of cattle
Storming across the plains.
At last I'm ready to do battle
Against the crows, the egrets and the cranes.

Or whatever high flying mysterious creatures
Threaten my domain.

Nickel Ice Cream

It is a world without why's and wherefores,
Nobody's world that is. Future is nowhere
Since yesterday got trapped behind iron doors.
And today, what's today but a prayer

Silencing nobody's fears. The moonlight
Has cast a shadow over oncoming years.
The locusts are wide-eyed, the August blight
Still dances wildly to any one's tears.

If winter comes soon, as surely it must,
If withering lilacs never revive,
Then even robots will turn into dust,
And only the apple and asp survive.

Good-bye to sweet nothing, good-bye to a dream
That melted away like a nickel ice cream.

Whimsy

When I sit alone and dream,
I don't feel old.
When I eat a chocolate bar.
Or dip a spoon in ice cream
When I see a falling star,
I don't feel old.

It isn't strength I need
To do what I want most.
I can summon all my will,
I can fashion a new creed,
And do battle with the frost,
      Yes, indeed.

I can think my white hair's black,
And my cheeks are tanned and smooth,
And my steps are quick and sure
As they were in my youth.
But I know I can't go back.
Ain't that the truth!

Florence Hackman cannot remember when she began writing. She does hope she knows when to stop. She spends her time on Cape Cod and in New Mexico.